I Know About™ Planets

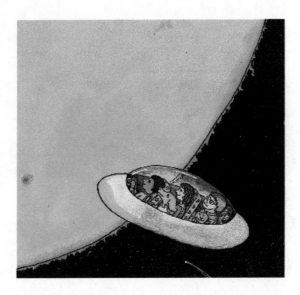

Written by Chris Jaeggi   Illustrated by Meyer Seltzer

Rand McNally for Kids™

Some planets are closer to the sun.
Some are farther away.

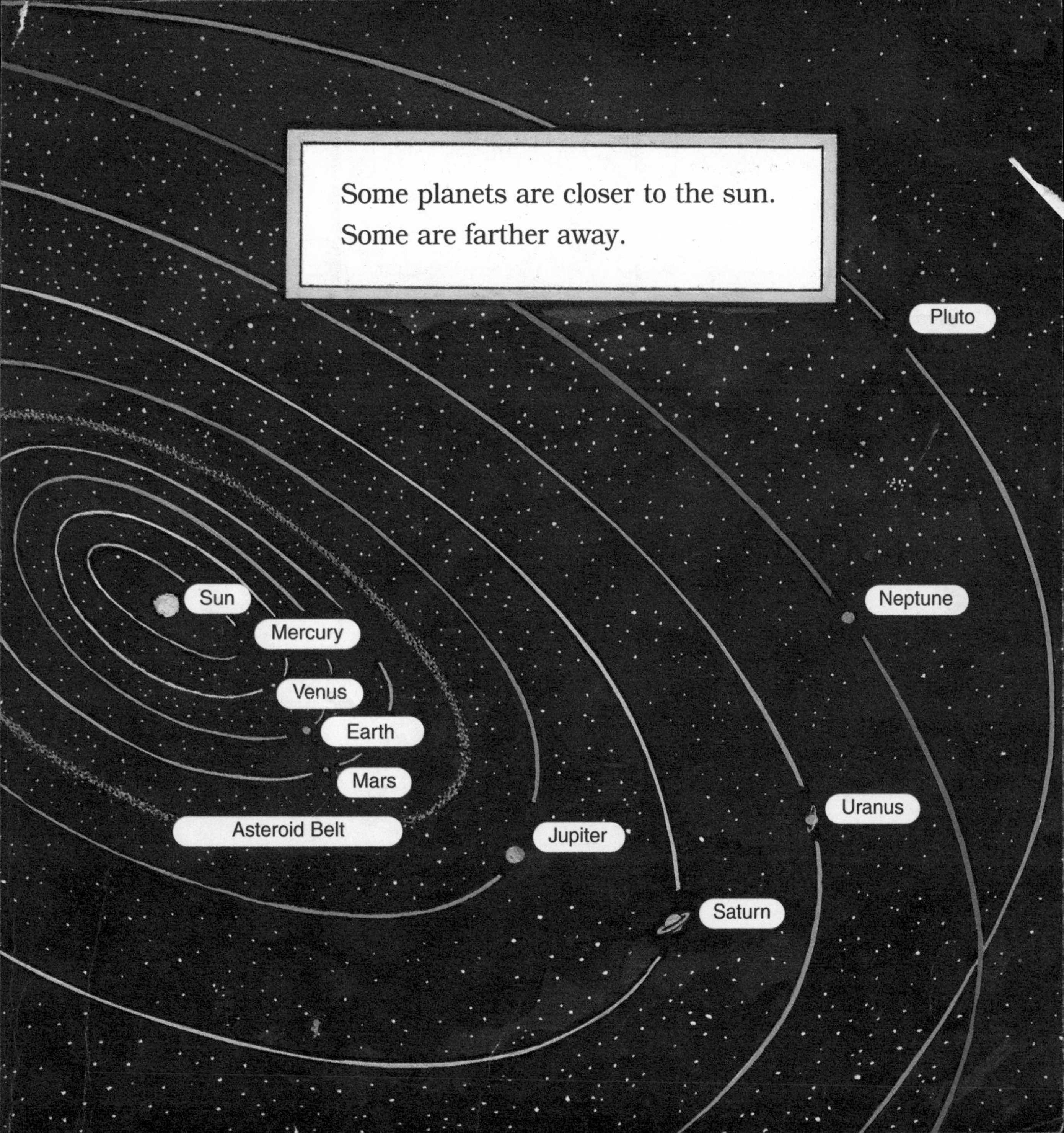

Pluto

Sun

Mercury

Venus

Earth

Mars

Asteroid Belt

Jupiter

Saturn

Uranus

Neptune

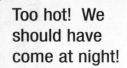

Too hot! We should have come at night!

That dark spot is a sun spot.

I hope our ship has sunblock on!

The sun is a star. Like all stars, it shines.
It's big and bright and hot. Very hot!
It gives us heat and light.

Pluto	·	−223° C	−369° F
Neptune	○	−216° C	−357° F
Uranus	⟆	−213° C	−351° F
Saturn	🪐	−178° C	−288° F
Jupiter	◯	−148° C	−234° F
Mars	●	−25° C	−13° F
Earth	●	14° C	58° F
Venus	●	464° C	867° F
Mercury	·	171° C	340° F
Sun		5704° C at surface	10,300° F at surface
		15 million° C at center	27 million° F at center

The planets that are close to the sun are warmer than those that are far away.

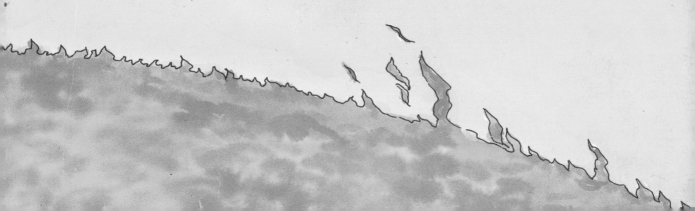

Mercury has no water on it and not much air,
but it does have a lot of large holes called craters.

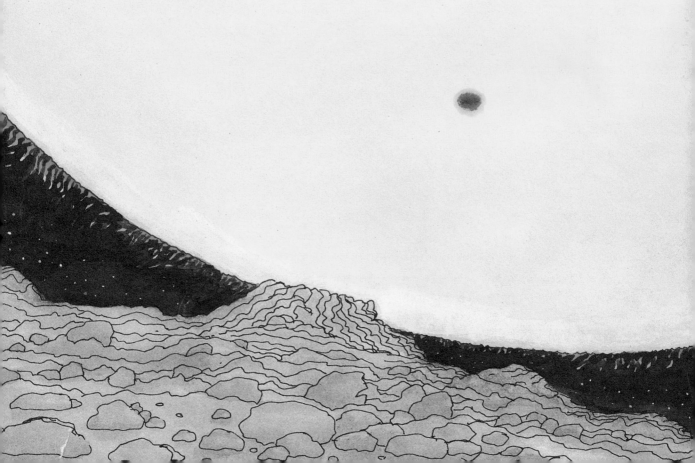

Venus is the hottest planet.
There are yellow clouds all around Venus.
They hold in the heat and block out the sun.

On Venus it's dark, like a cloudy, stormy day.
But it never rains on Venus.
It's dry, rocky, and dusty.

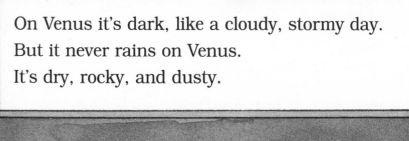

It's dangerous to come close.

The heat would fry us.

And Venus is so bright and pretty from Earth.

We live on the planet Earth.
It has blue water, brown and green land, and white clouds.
If you could look at Earth from space, it would look like this.

Mars is called the red planet because the ground on Mars is red.

Those moons look like two lumpy potatoes.

It's dry and windy on Mars.
The sky looks pink because of the red dust
that blows in the air.

Jupiter is the biggest of all the planets.
It has a Great Red Spot on it that is a giant,
swirling storm.

It's humongous!

The red spot
is bigger
than Earth!

Jupiter is made of gas, which means it doesn't have any land.
You couldn't walk on Jupiter because there isn't any ground to stand on.

Saturn has beautiful rings around its middle.
The rings are made of ice, rock, and dust.

Saturn has more moons than any other planet.

Uranus is a blue planet, and it has rings, too.
Uranus looks like it's tipped sideways.

Neptune is also a blue planet.
It has rings, too, but they're hard to see.

Pluto is the smallest of all the planets.

Planet Puzzler

 There are nine planets in all.

Can you name them?

The planets are round, like big balls.
Some are bigger. Some are smaller.

Find the biggest and
smallest planets.

The planets are different colors.

Which planets are blue?
Can you name the red planet?

Some planets have rings around them.

How many planets have rings?

Let's hurry home.
I'm hungry!

Didn't the astro-nuts
and Mars-mallows
fill you up?

I think you're
the astro-nut!